Chigwell and Loughton
in old picture postcards

by Stephen Pewsey

European Library ZALTBOMMEL/THE NETHERLANDS

Cover picture:
Buckhurst Hill post office in 1908.
The staff are assembled outside the
Queen's Road post office, opened
in 1892.

GB ISBN 90 288 6218 8 / CIP

© 1996 European Library – Zaltbommel/The Netherlands

No part of this book may be reproduced in any form, by print, photoprint,
microfilm or any other means, without written permission from the publisher.

Introduction

Settlers and invaders have passed through Chigwell and Loughton since prehistoric times. Deep in Epping Forest lies Loughton Camp – now tree-shrouded but once commanding extensive views – which served as a frontier fort for the local tribe during the Iron Age (500 B.C.-43 A.D.). The Romans tramped this way, building their road from London to Dunmow across Chigwell, with a bath-house and associated settlement at Little London, between Chigwell and Abridge. Saxon rule replaced Roman rule in the 5th century, and both Chigwell and Loughton have Anglo-Saxon names; Chigwell is 'the spring of someone named *Cicca*' and Loughton is 'the farm of *Luhha*', while Buckhurst Hill is 'the hill covered with beech-trees'. By the time of the Domesday Book (1087), the area was divided into ten separate estates, which would have comprised farmsteads, housing extended families and servants. Buckhurst Hill was part of the parish of Chigwell until 1895, when it became a separate urban district.

In the Middle Ages the area was dominated by the forest; at first known as the Forest of Essex, later as Waltham Forest, and later still as Epping Forest, the forest was a royal hunting preserve, with its own courts and officials to enforce the royal prerogative. Langfords or King's Place (demolished 1927) in Buckhurst Hill was a royal hunting lodge in the 14th century. Villagers did gain some benefits from living within the forest bounds; they were permitted to graze cattle on open land within the forest, and they were allowed to lop timber for firewood and for building. Farming was also important in the medieval period, as the area was fairly isolated; Loughton only had one main road, which led to Woodford. A road to Epping was not built until the 17th century, and the Epping New Road was constructed between 1830 and 1834. However, this isolation was an attraction for city merchants, seeking rural retreats near the city, and large houses for such men began to be built from the 16th century onwards. For a brief time, Loughton Hall was the centre of a glittering Jacobean social circle; lord of the manor Robert Wroth entertained James I there, and his daughter-in-law Mary Sidney was one of the first women novelists who moved in a literary coterie which included Ben Jonson.

The arrival of the railway in Loughton and Buckhurst Hill in 1856 immediately made the forest much more accessible, and it became a popular spot for weekend and bank holiday visits. The donkey rides and side shows that were set up to help the visitors spend their money were a cause of some annoyance, as indeed was the not infrequently rowdy behaviour of visitors. The poor of the East End poured into the forest, giving Loughton its gruesome nickname 'Lousy Loughton'. Housing followed the railway, and Buckhurst Hill in particular became quickly urbanised. Loughton retained something of a village-like atmosphere well into this century, while Chigwell remains predominantly rural in aspect.

Controversy over the forest split the communities during the 19th century. Piecemeal encroachment threatened to turn into full-scale developments as landowners purchased the Crown's forest rights. Hainault Forest, part of which lay in Chigwell, was disafforested in 1851 and the trees were removed. Such a fate also seemed to threaten Epping Forest, but the combined effect of local people (notably the Willingale family) defending their ancient right to lop wood in the forest, and court action to protect common rights, championed by the Corporation of London, was enough to save the forest from destruction. The passage of the Epping Forest Act of 1878 ensured that it would be permanently kept as an open space for public recreation, and Queen Victoria's visit to the forest in 1882 was greeted with immense local jubilation.

Buckhurst Hill became an urban district in 1895, as did Loughton in 1900. The two districts united with the parish of Chigwell in 1933 to form Chigwell Urban District, with the town hall in Old Station Road, Loughton.

Further local government changes in 1974 saw the creation of a much larger Epping Forest District, encompassing Epping, Waltham Abbey, Ongar and many small villages as well as the old Chigwell Urban District. Buckhurst Hill was already largely built up, but Loughton has grown steadily in the 20th century, notably along Alderton, Tycehurst and Spareleze Hills, where prestigious houses vie for views across the valley, and further east in Debden, where a huge new London County Council estate transformed the landscape after 1945.

Chigwell's main growth has been along 'Millionaire's Row' in Manor Road and also in Grange Hill, where the L.C.C.'s Hainault estate was built. In 1977 the opening of the M11 brought the area into the motorway age, but in a return to the ways of older times, it was agreed in 1994 to revive parish councils for Buckhurst Hill, Chigwell and Loughton, to bring the process of democracy nearer to the people.

Dickens once said of Chigwell, 'Chigwell my dear fellow is the greatest place in the world', and the whole area covered by this book largely remains a pleasant place to live, a scenic corner of Essex dotted with historic buildings, and much enhanced by the proximity of the majestic Epping Forest.

Acknowledgements

I would like to thank Essex County Libraries, Passmore Edwards Museum, and the Eclipse Archive for permission to use the images in this book. Thanks also go to Edwin Dare for advice during the initial stages of production, and to my wife Paulette, for her assistance throughout.

This book is dedicated to Alexander.

1   St. John's Church Buckhurst Hill.

This church was first built in 1837, and enlarged several times since. Buckhurst Hill formed part of the parish of Chigwell until 1867.

2   St. Mary's Church, Chigwell.

This postcard view dates from 1906. Little remains of the earliest, 12th-century church; in 1886 the old nave became the south aisle when a new, larger nave was built to the north. The pretty bell-tower with its shingled spire on the old nave dates back to about 1475.

3   St. Mary's Church, Chigwell.

This 1907 view shows the new nave added in 1886 very clearly. A number of distinguished worthies lie in the churchyard, including George Shillibeer (1797-1865), inventor of the omnibus.

4 St. John's Church, Loughton.

Consecrated in 1846, this church was built to replace the old parish church of St. Nicholas, which stood too far away from High Road to properly serve the residents of Loughton. The church is built in distinctive yellow brick and was designed in Norman style by Sydney Smirke. Although this 1906 view shows the church standing proud on its hilltop, it is now surrounded by tall trees and dense foliage.

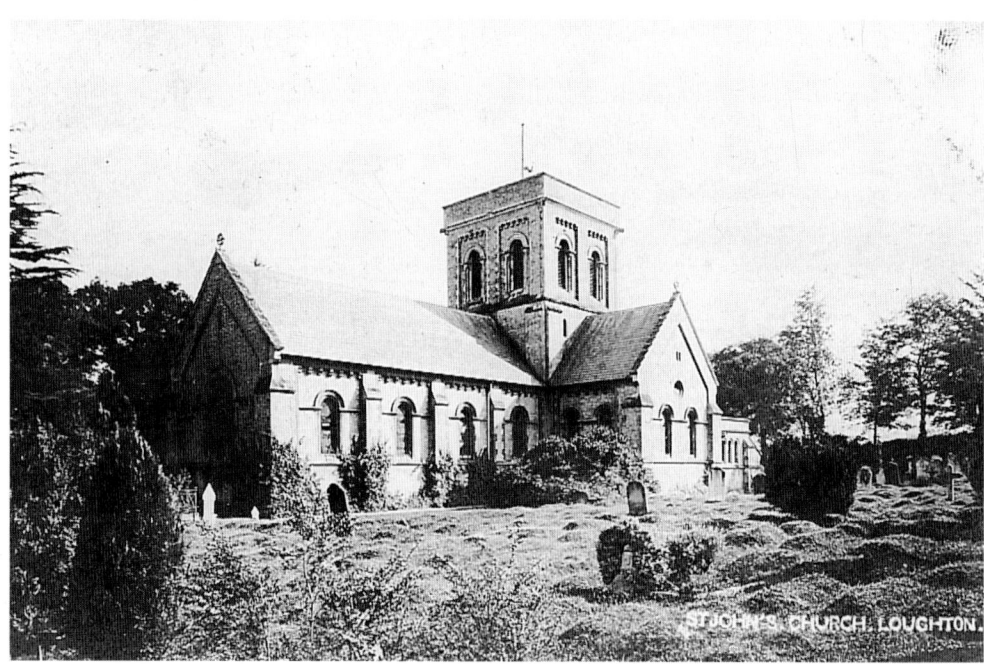

5 St. Mary's Church, Loughton.

Despite the building of St. John's, a town centre church was still needed for Loughton, and in 1871, St. Mary's was built as a chapel of ease. This simple but solid structure has thus been a Loughton landmark for well over a century.

THE PARISH CHURCH OF ST. MARY THE VIRGIN, LOUGHTON.

6 Tomb of Sarah Martin (1768-1826).

After St. John's Church, Loughton, was built, there was little further use for the old parish church of St. Nicholas, and it was dismantled, except for the chancel, which was finally demolished in 1877, only to be immediately rebuilt as a private chapel for Loughton Hall. One of the old tombs surviving in the churchyard is that of Sarah Martin, who wrote the well-known children's rhyme *Old Mother Hubbard*. At the age of 17, she refused an offer of marriage from Prince William (afterwards William IV), who had fallen madly in love with her!

7 All Saints', Chigwell Row.

This landmark church was first built in 1867, the tower being added in 1903 at a cost of almost £3,000. Built on land which was originally part of Hainault Forest, the church appears to be stone-built, but the stone is only cladding over a brick core. An unusual memorial in the churchyard is a wooden cross made from a First World War bomber propeller; this commemorates a Canadian airman.

8   Loughton Union Church.

The classical façade seen in this 1925 photograph has disappeared, and the trees have grown much taller, but a modern church still thrives on the site. First opened in 1813 as a Baptist chapel, the church now represents the united efforts of a number of nonconformist denominations.

9 Epping Forest.

Loughton in particular has long associations with Epping Forest. After determined attempts by local landlords to enclose and develop the forest, it was saved for the nation in 1878, when the Corporation of London took control of 5,000 acres of woodland and open space. Local people were prominent in defence of the forest and, more particularly, their ancient rights to lop firewood and graze their cattle in the forest.

10 Clay Ride, Loughton.

This track was cut through the forest from Baldwins Hill by Reverend J.W. Maitland, vicar of Loughton, lord of the manor and prominent in schemes to develop the forest.

11 School treat in Epping Forest.

After the opening of Epping Forest to the public, visitors poured in, particularly from London's East End, and on bank holidays the streets of Loughton were thronged with visitors on their way from the station to the forest. After the opening of Shaftesbury Retreat in Staples Road, huge parties of London children visited the forest, much to the annoyance of some residents. This postcard from 1909 shows a well-behaved party of picnicking schoolchildren.

12 Pond near Baldwins Hill.

This pleasant wooded scene, dating from 1957, appears to illustrate Baldwin's Pond, a popular fishing spot. Many of Epping Forest's ponds were created as a result of clay and gravel extraction.

13 Deer in Epping Forest.

At one time, red deer roamed Epping Forest, but they were hunted almost to extinction. The annual Epping Hunt had long been a boisterous day out for Londoners, but by the mid-19th century, it had become a disreputable affair. There are no longer any red deer, but fallow deer can still be seen deep in the woodland.

14 Dick Turpin's Cave.

The forest gave cover to many nefarious activities, most notably highway robbery, of whom the most famous practitioner was Dick Turpin (1705-39). His activities were romanticised in Harrison Ainsworth's novel *Rookwood*; Ainsworth invented the ride to York on Black Bess. Turpin certainly did use Epping Forest both for poaching and robbery, and a number of places were later claimed as the site of 'Dick Turpin's Cave', included a well-known inn at High Beach, now demolished.

15   A forest pool, Epping Forest.

A rather idealised sylvan scene; a whole series of prettified postcards like this were available as souvenirs for visitors to the forest. This view may show Golding's Pond on Golding's Hill at the turn of the century.

16 Alderton Hall, Loughton.

Chigwell and Loughton became rural retreats for city merchants as early as the 16th century, and still have a fine architectural heritage as a result. We look first at the oldest house in the area, Alderton Hall, seen here in a photograph from 1903. Referred to in the Domesday book as *Ælwartone*, it was one of eight manors of Loughton in 1086. The present building contains a 'great hall' of the 15th or 16th century, with many subsequent additions, including two wings, one of which was rebuilt in the 18th century.

17 North Farm, Loughton.

This is a 16th century building lying between Loughton and Buckhurst Hill. It was long associated with the construction company W. & C. French, founded by a Mrs. French in the last century. From small beginnings in Buckhurst Hill, French grew into an international corporation. The French family lived for many years at North Haven, next to North Farm. The former farmland associated with the farm has now been developed as the Great Woodcote Park housing estate.

18   Langfords, Kings Avenue, Buckhurst Hill.

Also known as King's Place and Potells. This was referred to in 1378 as 'the King's new lodge in Waltham Forest', showing that it was used as a hunting lodge. A farmhouse by the mid-19th century, Langford's was then converted into a residence suitable for a gentleman. In 1927, the house and grounds were sold for development, and Langfords was demolished; this photograph comes from the sales catalogue.

19 Chigwell Convent.

This grand building dates from the 18th century and was known as the Manor House. Today it is a Roman Catholic convent and school, run by the Sisters of the Sacred Hearts of Jesus and Mary.

20   Old wooden cottages, York Hill, Loughton.

These typical Essex weatherboarded cottages were demolished in 1892. Earlier they had been the original location of the *King's Head*, which now stands on the corner of High Road.

21 Priors, Traps Hill, Loughton.

This house and the adjacent Traps Hill House is largely 17th century, but was extensively altered in the 19th century. This view, from 1928, shows the oldest part of the house at the rear. There is a fine prospect over Loughton from the hilltop vantage point of this property.

22   Coulson's almshouses, Chigwell.

Believed to have been founded by one Thomas Coulson about 1557, these almshouses were rebuilt in 1858. They were originally built to house four poor widows of the parish. Chigwell School looms behind the cottages in this postcard view.

23 Luctons, Buckhurst Hill.

This was one of the oldest houses in Buckhurst Hill, dating back to the 16th or 17th century. This photograph dates from 1855, the year in which the property was purchased by Nathanael Powell, who added several large extensions to the house. Nathanael Powell was a partner in the Whitefriars Glass Works, which employed Burne-Jones as designer. A great local benefactor, Powell was Deputy Lieutenant of Essex. Following his death in 1906, Luctons was demolished and the grounds developed for housing. This photograph has a whimsical superimposition by one Mr. Cotton, showing himself on horseback on the lawn.

24   Holmehurst, Buckhurst Hill.

This view dates from about 1875. The lake, complete with rowing boat, can be seen at the foot of the picture, while Holmehurst crowns the hill. This large house is still in existence.

25 Church House, Church Lane, Loughton.

This house, which stands beside St. John's Church, was built in 1848 'with a view to give greater security to the Sacred Fabric and Graveyard'; it was built partly out of materials from the old St. Nicholas' Church.

26 Hawstead, Buckhurst Hill.

This large house, designed by H. Herbert Francis, stood next to Powell's Forest and Buckhurst Hill cricket ground, and is typical of the late Victorian mansions which once dotted this area. Demolished after the Second World War, its name is recalled in Hawsted, a lane which crosses its site.

27 Dr. Pendred's house, Loughton, High Road.

Now forming parts of the car showrooms of Brown's, this house was originally built about 1870 by architect Edmond Egan, but is best recalled by older residents as the surgery of Dr. Berthon Pendred, the local G.P. During the Second World War, it was requisitioned as Loughton's A.R.P. depot, being taken over as part of Brown's in 1947.

28   The *Roebuck*, Buckhurst Hill.

This inn name dates back to at least 1770, but the pub itself has been rebuilt several times. This photograph from 1890 shows the earlier inn, of which only a single gable (on the right in this picture) now survives. Note the sign on the left to the 'Ladies' Coffee Room and Tea Saloon'.

29 The Roebuck Hotel.

The present *Roebuck* was built in 1901, and is now a Forte hotel. This view from about 1960 shows Roebuck Green, a broad sward in front of the hotel which is part of Epping Forest.

30   The *Wheatsheaf*, York Hill, Loughton.

This pub stands next to the *King's Head* in York Hill. These original buildings were demolished in 1904-1905 to be replaced by the present inn.

31 The *King's Head*, Chigwell.

Immortalised as *The Maypole* in Charles Dickens' novel *Barnaby Rudge*, this inn dates back to at least the 17th century. This photograph dates from about 1875, before the timber beams were exposed, but the ancient overhanging jetties of each floor can clearly be seen. Dickens described the building as having 'more gable ends than a lazy man would care to count on a sunny day'!

32 Rear of the *King's Head*, Chigwell.

This postcard view of the back of the *King's Head* shows its pretty ornamental gardens. The various roof levels, ranges and windows of the inn show what enormous alteration it has undergone over the centuries.

33   Interior of the *King's Head*, Chigwell.

This is a rare view of the inside of the old hostelry. A sign on the staircase points up to the 'Chester Room'; used as a restaurant, this room retains its original 17th-century panelling.

34   The *Maypole*, Chigwell Row.

Although Dickens used the *King's Head* as the model for his inn in *Barnaby Rudge*, he took the name of the *Maypole* in Chigwell Row, and the descriptions of the scenery are from Chigwell Row rather than Chigwell. The original *Maypole* which Dickens knew lay behind this relatively modern building, and dated from the 15th century. It was earlier known as Skynners, and was demolished in the 1970s for modern housing.

35   The *Winston Churchill*, Rectory Lane.

Built after 1945, when the London County Council estate of Debden was created, this pub takes its name from the war-time Prime Minister, who was also the local M.P. from 1924 to 1945.

THE SIR WINSTON CHURCHILL, DEBDEN.

36 Samuel Harsnett (1561-1631).

Born in Colchester, Samuel Harsnett was vicar of Chigwell from 1597 until 1605, and later rose up through the church hierarchy to become Archbishop of York in 1629. It was in that year that he founded Chigwell School, in gratitude for his time at Chigwell, and, as he wrote, 'a mite of thankfulness to God, who from a poor vicar of this parish hath called me to my so high a dignity in his church'. This illustration shows the brass of Harsnett which is still on display in the parish church.

37 Dick Turpin (1705-1739).

England's most notorious highwayman was born in Hempstead in north Essex but had many associations with Epping Forest. He was reputed to have worked as a butcher in Buckhurst Hill in 1734, and also to have carried out a brutal robbery in Traps Hill, Loughton, where the widow Shelley was threatened with being roasted over her own fire if she refused to reveal where her valuables were hidden. Turpin also engaged in poaching within the forest, where he was reputed to have a hide-out; both Loughton Camp and the *Turpin's Cave* inn at High Beach were later claimed as the site of this hide-out, shown in this highly-romanticised engraving. Turpin was hanged at York.

38   William Higgins (1842-1870).

Though Epping Forest had been a royal hunting forest, by the 19th century, the Crown no longer had any interest in hunting, and sold the forest rights to the lord of the manor, W.W. Maitland, in 1857. His son, reverend J.W. Maitland, decided to inclose and develop the forest and, it was claimed, tried to deprive the Loughton folk of their ancient right to lop wood in the forest by inviting them to a feast on the night when lopping should have begun. Thomas Willingale, however, left the feast early to exercise his right, and a court case against him for lopping was dismissed in 1865. However, in 1866 his son Samuel and cousins Alfred Willingale and William Higgings were jailed for lopping. Higgins died young, it is said as a result of bad prison conditions. There was a national outcry over the prospect of Epping Forest's destruction, and in 1878 it was, through the Epping Forest Act, saved for the nation.

39   Chigwell School.

Founded in 1629 by Samuel Harsnett, Archbishop of York, this public school still thrives today over 350 years later. The building on the left is the original 17th century core of the school, and now serves as a library; the Georgian front of the head master's house can be seen on the right.

40 National Schools, Staples Road, Loughton.

Originating in 1761, this schoolhouse was built on York Green. The school, which was closely linked to the Church of England, was expanded throughout the 19th century until 1887, when Loughton School Board opened a new school on the south side of Staples Road. The National Schools closed in 1911, and the buildings were demolished in 1938-1939.

41 Loughton County High School for Girls.

This postcard view from 1913 shows the school laboratory. The school was opened in York Hill in 1906 and moved to Alderton Hill in 1908. The distinctive clock tower of the main building now forms part of Roding Valley High School.

42 Teyersons, butchers, Loughton.

A snowy view of this High Road butchers' shop, hung with carcases. Teyerson's, later Salter's, stood opposite the cricket ground on the edge of King's Green; a modern parade of shops now marks the site.

43 Sadler's stables.

This photograph from 1906 is a reminder of Loughton's rural past, and its dependence on passing horse traffic for much employment. Sadler's stood next to the old *Crown* inn, on a site later occupied by a service station and now a car park.

44   Hay carting in Chigwell Lane.

This photograph, which dates from before 1914, harks back to the times when the harvest was gathered in by hand, and when Chigwell Lane really was a country lane rather than the roaring motorway slip road it is today.

45 Chigwell Golf Club.

The clubhouse shown in this old postcard stands on an area formerly known as Sweeps Hill. The course stands on land between Chigwell High Road, Hainault Road, Manor Road and Forest Lane.

46   The Shaftesbury Retreat.

The Ragged School Union – later the Shaftesbury Society – began bringing groups of East End children on visits to Epping Forest in 1891, and the Shaftesbury Retreat in Loughton's Staples Road was the destination for most. Despite some local objections, these visits, sometimes several thousand strong, continued until the Second World War, in part funded by 'Pearson's Fresh Air Fund'. In this view, staff pose outside the headquarters building (now a private house), and beyond are large sheds, where meals were served.

47 Children's outing in Epping Forest.

This rare and undated photograph shows children enjoying a Fresh Air Fund outing in the forest. This charity was originally set up by a newspaper magnate to help poor children. Here a uniformed official appears to be blowing a whistle to marshall his charges. There were fears that the 'slum' children might spread lice and fleas, and as they were shepherded back to the station they were followed by a council cart spraying disinfectant! This led to Loughton's nickname 'Lousy Loughton'.

48 Lopping Hall.

When the Epping Forest Act was passed in 1878, part of its provision included the extinction of lopping rights. This was ironic, as the early struggle to save the forest from destruction by its owners revolved around the right to lop wood. In compensation, the new owners of the forest, the City of London, paid £7,000 to the people of Loughton, of which half was spent building Lopping Hall, a public hall to act as a social centre for the village. Lopping Hall was opened in 1884; this view shows the High Road frontage before 1933, when additional shops were built.

49 Loughton Cinema.

Loughton's own picture palace opened on the south side of the High Road in 1928. It was demolished in 1963 and a parade of shops now stands in its place.

50   Grange Farm Camp, Chigwell.

Grange Farm Camp was opened in 1951 offering a wide range of outdoor sporting and social activities. The swimming pool is seen here in this 1956 postcard, and there was also an athletics track and a camping ground. This last has been in use until quite recently, although the rest of the site has been abandoned and vandalised.

CH 25   SWIMMING POOL AND MAIN BUILDING, GRANGE FARM, CHIGWELL   A TUCK CARD

51　Buckhurst Hill Cricket Ground.

Buckhurst Hill Cricket Club, founded in 1864, is one of the oldest in Essex. The club still occupies its original ground beside Powell's Forest, almost surrounded by woodland, this ground being described by one commentator as 'one of the prettiest and best situated in the county'.

52 Chigwell Cricket Ground.

This cricket ground lay in the estate of Chigwell Hall. This grand house was built for the Savill family in 1876. The original moated manor house stood by the River Roding, where R.A.F. Chigwell later stood, itself later demolished to make way for the building of the M11 motorway in the 1970s.

53 Buckhurst Hill Village Hospital.

Buckhurst Hill's first hospital had comprised a couple of rooms in a High Road cottage. However, in 1868, a proper village hospital – seen here – was opened in Knighton Lane, which then was often called Hospital Lane. In 1912, Forest Hospital opened and the old village hospital became a convalescent home.

54 High Road, Buckhurst Hill.

This pleasant postcard view, which introduces a series of views of streets in the area, looks east along the High Road. Palmerston Road can be seen on the right, and a horse-drawn cart is the only traffic. The avenue of chestnut trees fronting the green still stands, much to the delight of local children each autumn.

55 Queen's Road, Buckhurst Hill.

Queen's Road is Buckhurst Hill's main shopping thoroughfare, and this view from about 1960 shows the lower end. Queen's Road was first laid out in 1856-1857.

56 Gladstone Road, Buckhurst Hill.

This road, and Palmerston and Westbury Roads were all made up in 1868, though Gladstone Road was not adopted until 1883. This photograph, taken from the Russell Road end in 1925, shows the neat terraces of red-brick houses which characterise much of this part of Buckhurst Hill.

57 Church Green, Buckhurst Hill.

The spire of St. John's Church peeps out above the trees, while in the foreground is Top Pond, earlier known as Wooder's Pond after Reuben Wooder, who owned land hereabouts. The pond lies nearly opposite the *Bald Faced Stag* (recently renamed 'Jeffersons'!), a forest inn which dates back to at least the 18th century.

THE POND AND ST. JOHN'S CHURCH, BUCKHURST HILL.   BH.6

**58   Roebuck Lane,
Buckhurst Hill.**

The *Roebuck* lies at the top of this road, which in 1928, when this photograph was taken, still had a very rural aspect. Nowadays it is lined with substantial houses, but is still tree-lined.

59   Vicarage Lane, Chigwell.

One of Chigwell's most ancient lanes, Vicarage Lane appears in records as far back as 1492. It has a very rural aspect in this pre-1905 photograph.

60 High Road, Chigwell.

Two children pose outside Dawkins, for many years Chigwell's post office and village shop, but now a private house. Beyond lies the entrance to Radley's builders' yard, which is still in existence.

61 Forest Lane, Chigwell.

This road, adjoining Chigwell Golf Gourse, is lined with prestigious houses; this area is popularly known as 'Millionaires' Row'!

Forest Lane, Chigwell.
FRITH CGW.99

62 High Road, Loughton.

This view from about 1900, shows the junction with Station Road, with Dr. Pendred's house on the left. The turreted waiting room which was added to the original building can be seen at the extreme left. The turret and roof of Lopping Hall are prominent landmarks.

Nº 63 →

63   High Road, Loughton.

This photograph pre-dates the building of Lopping Hall (opened in 1884), and shows the junction of High Road and Station Road. The drinking fountain was erected about 1870, complete with improving biblical verses carved over the arches, but was knocked down by a bus in a fog in 1934, and rebuilt in timber two years later. The shop was Hutchin's pharmacy, which is still on the site to this day.

64 High Road, Loughton.

This 1876 photograph was taken outside St. Mary's Church looking south-west. The post office is on the right, while across Forest Road is a substantial brick building. This is Loughton's police station, built between 1860 and 1864 and replaced with a modern building in 1963.

65 High Road, Loughton.

This postcard looks in the opposite direction to the previous view. St. Mary's Church and Dr. Pendred's house are on the right, with Loughton's first post office on the left at the junction of High Road and Forest Road. The post office later moved round the corner to a building in Forest Road, and later still back into the High Road. These last premises have now been converted into a public house, appropriately named the *Last Post*.

St. Mary's Loughton.

66   High Road, Loughton.

Forest Road lies on the left, and the post office can be seen at the junction. The house behind acted as the local telephone exchange. Beyond was Blow's, the baker, and then Cuthbert's, builder's merchant.

67 Church Hill, Loughton.

Taken in 1904, this photograph looks towards the *Plume of Feathers*, the sign of which can be seen in the distance. The timber houses, including Howe's wheelwright's works – its front yard littered with carts – have long been swept away and replaced with the Marjorams housing estate.

68 Traps Hill, Loughton.

Monghyr Cottage, a solid early 19th-century house (now in use as offices), stands on the left. This view dates from 1877. Opposite, local corn merchant George Gould built a massive house, Brooklyn, in 1888, where Loughton library now stands. According to local legend, the ghost of Dick Turpin rides down this hill with the ghost of Widow Shelley, whom he robbed in Traps Hill, clinging to his back!

69   York Hill, Loughton.

King's Green, seen in the foreground, was earlier known as Cage Green, as it was once the site of the village lock-up. York Hill was earlier known as Mutton Row or Black Mutton Row, 'black mutton' being a euphemism for poached venison. It was named York Hill in 1852 after Frederick, Duke of York, who is supposed to have had an affair with Mary Anne Clarke, a courtesan who lived in Loughton Lodge.

70 Loughton from Alderton Hill.

This postcard from 1930 is a reminder of just how rural Loughton once was. Cows grace peacefully in fields where the smart houses of Alderton Hill and Spareleaze Hill now stand. The spire of Lopping Hall is prominent in the distance.

71 Church Lane, Loughton.

Church Lane was earlier known as Blind Lane. The roadway is overhung with trees which obscure the view of St. John's Church. Church House is on the right.

72 Debden.

Debden was all fields until 1945. The owner of the land, Commander J.W. Maitland, sold the estate, including Loughton Hall, to the London County Council, and over the next ten years, nearly four thousand houses were built, complete with shopping parade (The Broadway) and industrial estate, where the Bank of England Printing Works was the largest employer.

73 Borders Lane, Debden.

A row of shops about 1955. Border's Lane was earlier known as Church Lane, and took its name from Border's Farm, demolished in the building of the Debden estate.

74 The White Bridge.

Before 1890, there was no road link between the Loughton and Chigwell side of the Roding. However, in that year Roding Lane was built. The White Bridge was one of two ancient footbridges, the other being Loughton Bridge (now part of Chigwell Lane).

75 Buckhurst Hill Station.

The Eastern Counties Railway (later the Great Eastern) was extended from Woodford to Loughton in 1856, with this intermediate station at Buckhurst Hill. The line was extended to Epping and Ongar in 1865, and a loop line to Ilford via Hainault and Chigwell was added in 1903.

STATION. BUCKHURST HILL.

76 **Staff at Buckhurst Hill Station.**

Taken about 1885, this photograph shows the two-storey station-house, with staff resplendent in their Great Eastern uniforms ranged along the down platform.